# Night Skies

## Variables, Expressions, and Equations

**Dawn McMillan**

## Publishing Credits

**Editor**
Sara Johnson

**Editorial Director**
Dona Herweck Rice

**Editor-in-Chief**
Sharon Coan, M.S.Ed.

**Creative Director**
Lee Aucoin

**Publisher**
Rachelle Cracchiolo, M.S.Ed.

## Image Credits

The author and publisher would like to gratefully credit or acknowledge the following for permission to reproduce copyright material: cover NASA; p.1 NASA; p.3 Shutterstock; p.4 Photolibrary.com/David Parker; p.5 Photolibrary.com/Julian Baum; p.6 Photolibrary.com/Martin Kornmesser; p.7 Photolibrary.com/Gerard Fritz; p.8 Photolibrary.com; p.9 Photolibrary.com/Chris Butler; p.10 NASA, Shutterstock (background); p.11 Photolibrary.com/Eckhard Slawik; p.12 NASA; p.13 (left) Alamy, (right) Big Stock Photo; p.14 Photolibrary.com; p.15 Photolibrary.com; p.16 NASA; p.17 NASA; p.18 NASA; p.19 Photolibrary.com; p.20 NASA, (inset) Photolibrary.com; p.21 Corbis/Tim Klusalaas; p.22 Rob Cruse; p.23 Shutterstock; pp.24–26 Rob Cruse; p.27 Shutterstock; p.29 Shutterstock

While every care has been taken to trace and acknowledge copyright, the publishers tender their apologies for any accidental infringement where copyright has proved untraceable. They would be pleased to come to a suitable arrangement with the rightful owner in each case.

## *Teacher Created Materials*

5301 Oceanus Drive
Huntington Beach, CA 92649-1030
http://www.tcmpub.com

**ISBN 978-0-7439-0912-9**
© 2009 Teacher Created Materials, Inc.
Made in China
Nordica.012016.CA21501561

# Table of
# Contents

A Visit to the Planetarium    4

Our Solar System    6

The Inner Planets    8

The Outer Planets    16

Making a Model    21

Problem-Solving Activity    28

Glossary    30

Index    31

Answer Key    32

# A Visit to the Planetarium

Last night, Dad and I visited the **planetarium** (plan-uh-TAIR-ee-uhm). A planetarium is like a theater with a big domed ceiling. People learn about the stars and the planets there. A special projector shows images of the night sky on the roof above.

Dad and I took our seats. Suddenly it was dark and we were on a tour of the night sky. We learned that all of the stars we see in the night sky are part of our **galaxy**. Our galaxy is called the Milky Way. Our **solar system** is part of the Milky Way. It can be found toward the Milky Way's edge.

The show lasted 35 minutes. But, there was also a bonus feature after the show. That was a fun surprise.

I enjoyed seeing the stars in the Milky Way at the planetarium. But what interested me most was our solar system. An **astronomer** (uh-STRON-uh-mer) at the planetarium told me more about it.

## LET'S EXPLORE MATH

**Variables** (VAIR-ee-uh-buhls) are letters or symbols that can be used to **represent** numbers. An **expression** is a group of symbols or numbers that can stand for a number or quantity. It does not have an equal sign.

An expression can be written to show the total number of minutes spent watching the presentation in the planetarium. Here is the expression: $35 + x$

a. What does the 35 represent?

b. What does the $x$ represent?

# Our Solar System

At the planetarium, I learned that the main part of our solar system consists of the sun and 8 planets. The planets are Mercury, Venus, Earth, Mars, Jupiter, Saturn, Uranus, and Neptune.

There are at least 3 **dwarf planets** and over 150 moons in our solar system as well. There are also many other things such as **asteroids**, **meteoroids**, and **comets**.

## Not a Planet!

In 1930, scientists thought they had discovered a new planet. They named this planet Pluto. But in 2006, it was decided that Pluto is a dwarf planet. It is not big enough to be called a planet.

sun

Mercury
Venus
Earth
Mars
Jupiter
Saturn
Uranus
Neptune

The sun and 8 planets in our solar system

# The Sun

The sun is an enormous star that is at least 4.6 billion years old. It is the center of our solar system.

The sun's **gravity** is very powerful. This means each planet is pulled toward the sun. At the same time, each planet's motion moves it away from the sun. The balance between the sun's pull and a planet's motion makes the planet orbit the sun.

## Giver of Life

The energy from the sun gives Earth both light and heat. Without the sun, there would be no life on Earth!

# The Inner Planets

Our solar system consists of 4 inner planets and 4 outer planets. The inner planets are Mercury, Venus, Earth, and Mars. The outer planets are Jupiter, Saturn, Uranus, and Neptune.

The inner planets are rocky, with solid surfaces. They are often hit by asteroids. This creates many large craters on their surfaces.

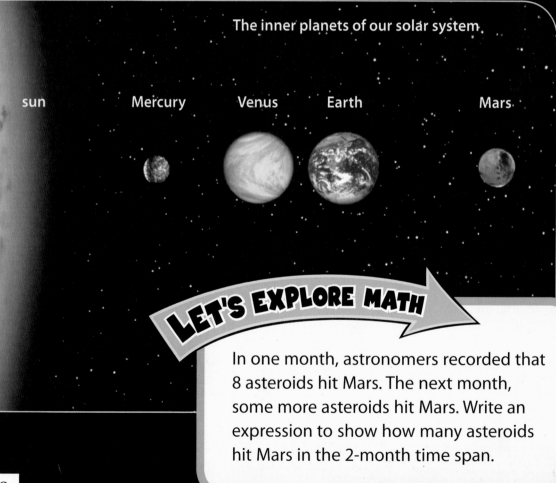

The inner planets of our solar system

sun　　Mercury　　Venus　　Earth　　Mars

## LET'S EXPLORE MATH

In one month, astronomers recorded that 8 asteroids hit Mars. The next month, some more asteroids hit Mars. Write an expression to show how many asteroids hit Mars in the 2-month time span.

# Mercury

Mercury is the closest planet to the sun. It is just over $^1/_3$ of the size of Earth.

A year on any planet is the time it takes the planet to make 1 orbit around the sun. Mercury orbits quickly around the sun. It only takes 88 Earth days for Mercury to orbit the sun.

A day on any planet is the time it takes to make 1 **rotation** (row-TAY-shuhn) on its axis. Mercury rotates very slowly. One day on Mercury is equal to 176 Earth days. That means you would have to stay up for 176 days on Earth to experience one day on Mercury!

sun

Mercury

## Hot and Cold

Temperatures on Mercury can get as high as 860°F (460°C) and as low as −356°F (−180°C).

9

# Venus

My favorite planet is Venus. Venus is the second planet from the sun. It is 95% of the size of Earth. It is sometimes called Earth's "sister planet" because the two planets are so similar in size.

Venus is actually hotter than Mercury is, even though it is over 31 million miles (50 million km) farther from the sun. It reaches temperatures of 900°F (482°C)!

## That's Hot!

An **equation** is a mathematical sentence that shows 2 equal numbers or quantities. It is written with an equal sign. I could write an equation to figure out how much hotter Venus is than Mercury.

$x = 482°C - 460°C$

Venus is 22°C hotter than Mercury!

sun

Venus

Venus is the nearest planet to Earth, so we can see it with our eyes. It looks like a bright star. It is the brightest thing in the night sky apart from the moon. Sometimes we can see Venus in the sky just before sunrise. At other times we can see it just after sunset.

On average, Venus passes between Earth and the sun twice every 121.5 years. This is called the Transit of Venus. The last Transit of Venus was in 2004. The next is due on June 6, 2012. After that, it will not happen again until 2117.

## The Transit of Venus

The equation $2117 - 2012 = y$ could be used to find how many years will pass between these two Transits of Venus. I will be 15 in 2012. Is it probable that I will be alive to see the Transit of Venus in 2117?

105 years pass between the 2 transits. It is not probable that you will be alive.

sun

Venus

# Earth

Earth is the largest of the inner planets. It has plenty of oxygen in the air, and 71% of its surface is covered with water. This is why it is the only planet in our solar system that supports life—that we know of.

The distance between the sun and Earth is around 93 million miles (150 million km). That is about 2½ times farther from the sun than Mercury is.

## How Much of Earth Is Land?

I know that 71% of Earth is water. So the rest of Earth, $x$, must be land. I can show that using the equation:

$71\% + x = 100\%$

I can find the percentage of land by solving for $x$.

$100\% - 71\% = x$

$100\% - 71\% = 29\%$

That means only 29% of Earth is land!

The **atmosphere** (AT-muhs-fear) of Earth is made of 77% **nitrogen** and 21% oxygen. There are also very small amounts of **carbon dioxide** and other gases.

The Earth's surface temperature varies. The North and South Poles can be at temperatures far below freezing. Yet temperatures in some desert areas can get up to 134°F (57°C).

## LET'S EXPLORE MATH

The ice caps in the polar regions contain nearly 90% of all the fresh water on Earth. An equation can be used to find the percentage of Earth's fresh water that is not in the ice caps.

Solve for $x$ to make this mathematical equation true: $90\% + x = 100\%$

The Earth rotates on its axis. This axis is tilted. When the North Pole leans towards the sun, most of the sun's light falls on the Northern Hemisphere. So it is summer in the north and winter in the south. Six months later the South Pole leans towards the sun. The seasons are the other way around then.

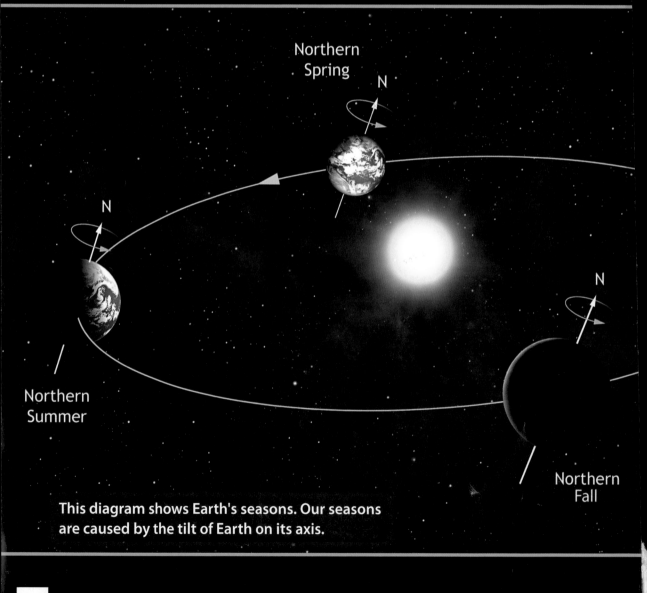

Northern Spring

N

N

Northern Summer

N

Northern Fall

**This diagram shows Earth's seasons. Our seasons are caused by the tilt of Earth on its axis.**

# Mars

Mars is the last planet in the inner solar system. It is nearly 142 million miles (229 million km) from the sun, and about 49 million miles (79 million km) from Earth.

The surface of Mars is very rocky, and it is covered with red soil. It has the highest mountain in the solar system, Olympus Mons. The mountain is 16.8 miles (27 km) high, or 3 times as high as Mount Everest!

orthern
Winter          N

## How High Is Mt. Everest?

The equation
$16.8 \div 3 = x$
will help me figure it out!

5.6 miles high

## Inner Planet Distances from the Sun

| Planet | Distance | |
|---|---|---|
| | **Miles** | **Kilometers** |
| Mercury | 35,983,093 | 57,909,175 |
| Venus | 67,237,912 | 108,208,930 |
| Earth | 92,955,819 | 149,597,890 |
| Mars | 141,633,262 | 227,936,640 |

# The Outer Planets

At the planetarium, I also learned about the planets in the outer solar system. These are Jupiter, Saturn, Uranus, and Neptune. These planets are called gas giants. This is because they are made mostly of gases. None of these planets has a solid surface, only a thick atmosphere. This atmosphere becomes thicker the closer it gets to the planet's **core**.

The outer planets of our solar system

Jupiter        Saturn       Uranus    Neptune

## Outer Planet Distances from the sun

| Planet | Distance | |
|---|---|---|
| | **Miles** | **Kilometers** |
| Jupiter | 483,682,805 | 778,412,020 |
| Saturn | 886,526,063 | 1,426,725,400 |
| Uranus | 1,783,939,419 | 2,870,972,200 |
| Neptune | 2,795,084,767 | 4,498,252,899 |

# Jupiter

Jupiter is the largest planet in our solar system. Even though it is about 484 million miles (779 million km) from the sun, Jupiter is the second brightest planet in our night sky. I was amazed to find out that Jupiter has 63 moons!

Jupiter is mainly made up of gases. But its center may have a small, solid core. The temperature of the core might be about 54,000°F (29,982°C).

Great Red Spot

## Storms on Jupiter

One of Jupiter's most famous features is the Great Red Spot. This is an enormous storm, up to 28,000 miles (45,062 km) wide by 8,700 miles (14,001 km) long.

Saturn is the second largest planet in the solar system. It is around 887 million miles (1,427 million km) from the sun. It is most famous for its spectacular rings.

Winds on Saturn can reach speeds of 1,100 miles (1,770 km) per hour. That is 5 ½ times faster than the most powerful tornadoes on Earth!

## Solid Center

At the very center of Saturn, we would find a solid core about the size of Earth.

# Uranus

Uranus is much smaller than Jupiter and Saturn are. Yet it is over 4 times bigger than Earth is. It is nearly 1,800 million miles (2,897 million km) farther away from the sun than Earth is.

The temperature in the clouds of Uranus is −417°F (−214°C). Its core temperature is thought to be about 12,600°F (6,982°C).

## LET'S EXPLORE MATH

When writing an expression or equation, it is important to look for key words that tell which opertion to use.

**a.** Mercury is about ⅓ the size of Earth. If the size of Earth is represented by $e$, which expression best shows the size of Mercury?

**1.** $\frac{1}{3} - e$    **2.** $\frac{1}{3} e$    **3.** $\frac{1}{3} \div e$    **4.** $\frac{1}{3} + e$

**b.** Uranus is about 4 times bigger than Earth. If Earth is represented by $e$, which expression best shows the size of Uranus?

**1.** $4 \div e$    **2.** $4 + e$    **3.** $4e$    **4.** $4 - e$

# Neptune

Neptune is the last of the gas giants, and the farthest away from the sun. It takes Neptune 165 Earth years to orbit the sun once because it is over 2 billion miles (3 billion km) away!

Neptune was discovered in 1846. It will not complete the orbit it was in then until 2011!

## Cold Volcanoes?

Triton, the largest moon of Neptune, is the coldest thing so far discovered in the solar system. It has volcanoes that send out pink snow instead of molten rock.

# Making a Model

My visit to the planetarium gave me the idea of making a model of the solar system. I wanted the planets in my model to be in proportion to their original sizes. Obviously, my model couldn't be life-size! I would have to figure out a **scale**.

The planets in our solar system

Dad and I found a great website on the Internet. It gives the diameter of each planet and the sun.

We found some of the things we would need around the house. Then, we bought the polystyrene (pol-ee-STY-reen) rings, balls, and board at a craft shop. Soon we had gathered all the things we needed for our model. But we could not make a model of the sun. Its diameter was just too big!

## Materials

- paints
- paintbrushes
- strong glue
- 2 polystyrene rings
- polystyrene balls
- modeling clay
- wire (8 pieces)
- 1 polystyrene display board

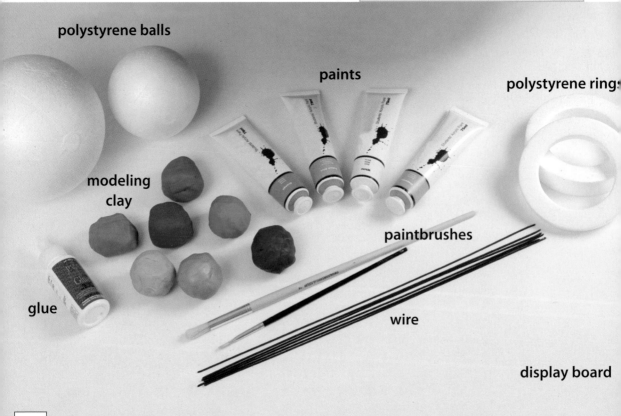

polystyrene balls

paints

polystyrene rings

modeling clay

paintbrushes

glue

wire

display board

Here is the chart that we used to make sure our model was proportional. Our scale made sure that the planets were in proportion to their original sizes. Our scale was 1 mm = 1,000 kilometers.

| Star/Planet | Actual Diameter (km) | Reduced Diameter of Ball (mm) | Color |
|---|---|---|---|
| Mercury | 4,900 | 4.9 | gray |
| Venus | 12,100 | 12.1 | orange |
| Earth | 12,700 | 12.7 | blue and green |
| Mars | 6,700 | 6.7 | red |
| Jupiter | 142,000 | 142 | white |
| Saturn | 120,000 | 120 | blue with red and pink stripes |
| Uranus | 51,800 | 51.8 | pink |
| Neptune | 49,500 | 49.5 | blue |

**Molding the clay and painting the polystyrene balls**

**Mercury is being put onto a piece of wire.**

First, we painted the polystyrene balls for the larger planets. Then we molded the different colored clay into balls for the smaller planets. Then we glued a ring around the ball representing Saturn.

Students' Acrylic Paint 75ml

To put the model together, we started with Mercury. We took some wire and stuck it into the bottom of the clay ball. Then we put some glue on the other end of the wire and stuck the wire into the display board. The glue made sure it did not fall out.

Then we placed all the other planets in their correct positions. It really looked like the actual solar system!

**LET'S EXPLORE MATH**

There are 8 planets in the solar system. Dad and I are using polystyrene balls to represent 2 of the planets. The rest of the planets will be made of modeling clay.

a. Use the variable $c$ to write an equation to show how many planets will be made of clay.

b. Solve the equation you wrote for problem **a**.

When all the planets were placed on the display
board and all glue had dried, our model was finished.
The planet sizes are to scale, but their distances are not!

I was going to put the model in my bedroom. But
Dad likes it so much, we put it on the living room table.
It looks great!

It has been fun learning about the solar system. I think I would like to be an astronomer when I grow up.

In the meantime, I am looking forward to learning more about our solar system.

A spiral galaxy

## Space Discovery

Astronomers have just discovered a new solar system in a distant galaxy. It has six planets orbiting around a sun. Some of the planets are about the size of Earth. Others are much larger. And this new solar system has a combined total of 30 moons!

The table below is missing some of the current information astronomers have learned about this new solar system.

### Planets in New Solar System

| Name of Planet | Approximate Diameter (miles) | Number of Moons |
|----------------|------------------------------|-----------------|
| Zenner | $z$ | 1 |
| Xenox | 3,000 | $x$ |
| Axiom | $a$ | 2 |
| Centaur | 75,000 | $c$ |
| Yukka | 36,000 | 17 |

## Solve It!

For each question below, write mathematical equations using variables to help you figure out the answers.

**a.** Xenox has 15 fewer moons than Yukka. How many moons does Xenox have?

**b.** Centaur has 6 more moons than Axiom. How many moons does Centaur have?

Centaur's diameter is 68,500 miles bigger than Zenner's diameter. Axiom's diameter and Xenox's diameter total 4,000 miles.

**c.** What are the diameters of planets Zenner and Axiom?

Use the steps below to help you solve the problems above.

**Step 1:** Use the information in the table to write question **a.** as a mathematical equation. Then solve your equation.

**Step 2:** Use the information in the table to write question **b.** as a mathematical equation. Then solve your equation.

**Step 3:** Use the information in the table and above question **c.** to write mathematical equations. Then solve your equations.

# Glossary

**asteroids**—pieces of rock left over from the formation of the solar system about 4.6 billion years ago

**astronomer**—a person who studies objects and matter outside Earth's atmosphere

**atmosphere**—the mass of gases surrounding a planet

**carbon dioxide**—a type of greenhouse gas formed naturally and by the impact of human activities

**comets**—bright celestial bodies with cloudy tails that move in an orbit around the sun

**core**—the center part of a planet or a star

**dwarf planets**—objects in space, such as Pluto, that orbit the sun and look like, but are smaller than, our solar system's planets

**equation**—a mathematical sentence that shows 2 equal numbers or quantities; written with an equal sign

**expression**—a group of symbols or numbers standing for a number or quantity; a mathematical phrase without an equal sign

**galaxy**—a massive group of stars, dust, and gas held together by gravity

**gravity**—a force that pulls things toward each other

**meteroids**—stone-like or metal-like material traveling through space

**nitrogen**—a type of colorless gas

**planetarium**—a place where images of the solar system are projected onto a special ceiling

**represent**—stand in place of; to stand for

**rotation**—the act of turning, or rotating, on an axis or center

**scale**—the ratio between the size of the drawing and what is represented

**solar system**—the part in space that is made up of all the planets that orbit the sun, including moons, comets, asteroids, and meteoroids

**variables**—symbols or letters representing unknown values

# Index

asteroids, 6, 8

astronomer, 5, 27

atmosphere, 13, 16

axis, 9, 14

comets, 6

core, 16, 17, 18

craters, 8

dwarf planets, 6

Earth, 6, 7, 8, 9, 10, 11, 12–14, 15, 18, 19, 23

equations, 10, 11, 12, 13, 15

expressions, 5, 8, 19

galaxy, 4

gases, 13, 16, 17, 20

gravity, 7

Great Red Spot, 17

inner planets, 8–15

Internet, 22

Jupiter, 6, 8, 16, 17, 19, 23

Mars, 6, 8, 15, 23

Mercury, 6, 8, 9, 10, 12, 15, 19, 23, 25

meteoroids, 6

Milky Way, 4, 5

moons, 6, 11, 17, 20

Mount Everest, 15

Neptune, 6, 8, 16, 20, 23

Olympus Mons, 15

orbit, 7, 9, 20

outer planets, 8, 16–20

planetarium, 4–5, 6, 16, 21

Pluto, 6

proportional model, 21–26

rotation, 9

Saturn, 6, 8, 16, 18, 19, 23, 24

seasons, 14

solar system, 4, 5, 6–7, 8, 12, 16, 17, 18, 21, 25, 27

stars, 4, 5, 11

sun, 6, 7, 9, 10, 11, 12, 15, 16, 17, 18, 19, 20, 22, 23

temperatures, 9, 10, 13, 17, 19

Transit of Venus, 11

Uranus, 6, 8, 16, 19, 23

variables, 5, 10, 11, 12, 15

Venus, 6, 8, 10–11, 15, 23

volcanoes, 20

## Let's Explore Math

**Page 5:**

**a.** 35 represents the number of minutes of the original show.

**b.** $X$ represents the number of minutes the bonus feature lasted.

**Page 8:**

$8 + x$

**Page 13:**

$90\% + x = 100\%$

$x = 10\%$, so 10% of Earth's fresh water is not in the ice caps.

**Page 19:**

**a.** **2.** $\frac{1}{3} e$

**b.** **3.** $4 e$

**Page 25:**

**a.** $2 + c = 8$

**b.** $2 + c = 8$

$8 - 2 = c$

$c = 6$

6 planets will be made of clay.

## Problem-Solving Activity

**a.** $17 - 15 = x$

$17 - 15 = 2$ moons

Xenox has 2 moons.

**b.** $2 + 6 = c$

$2 + 6 = 8$ moons

Centaur has 8 moons.

**c.** $75{,}000 - 68{,}500 = z$

$75{,}000 - 68{,}500 = 6{,}500$ miles in diameter

Zenner has a diameter of 6,500 miles.

$3{,}000 + a = 4{,}000$

$4{,}000 - 3{,}000 = a$

$4{,}000 - 3{,}000 = 1{,}000$ miles in diameter

Axiom has a diameter of 1,000 miles.